SERVING IN YOUR CHURCH NURSERY

OTHER TITLES IN THE ZONDERVAN PRACTICAL MINISTRY GUIDE SERIES

Serving in Your Church Music Ministry, Randall D. Engle
Serving as a Church Greeter, Leslie Parrott
Serving as a Church Usher, Leslie Parrott
Serving in Your Church Prayer Ministry, Charles E. Lawless Jr.
Serving in Church Visitation, Jerry M. Stubblefield
Serving by Safeguarding Your Church, Robert H. Welch

Paul E. Engle is an executive editor and associate publisher for editorial development at Zondervan. He has served as a pastor and as an instructor in several seminaries. Among the eight books he has written are *Baker's Wedding Handbook*, *Baker's Funeral Handbook*, and *God's Answers for Life's Needs*.

Julia A. Spohrer is director of children and family ministries at Valley Community Baptist Church in Avon, Connecticut. She has also served in churches in Ohio, Illinois, and New York. She holds degrees in Christian and religious education from Columbia Bible College and Trinity Evangelical Divinity School. She earned her Ed.D. in educational leadership from The Southern Baptist Theological Seminary in Louisville, Kentucky.

SERVING IN YOUR CHURCH NURSERY

PAUL E. ENGLE, SERIES EDITOR
JULIA A. SPOHRER

ZONDERVAN™

GRAND RAPIDS, MICHIGAN 49530 USA

ZONDERVAN™

Serving in Your Church Nursery
Copyright © 2003 by Julia A. Spohrer

Requests for information should be addressed to:
Zondervan, *Grand Rapids, Michigan 49530*

Library of Congress Cataloging-in-Publication Data

Spohrer, Julia A., 1970-
    Serving in your church nursery / Julia A. Spohrer.
        p. cm. — (Zondervan practical ministry guides)
      ISBN 0-310-24104-9
    1. Christian education of preschool children. I. Title. II. Series.
BV1539.S66   2003
259'.22—dc21

                                        2003005035

Interior design by Sherri L. Hoffman

Printed in the United States of America

---

03 04 05 06 07 08 09 /❖ DC/ 10 9 8 7 6 5 4 3 2 1

CONTENTS

A LETTER TO THE READER

Dear friend in ministry,
I wish we could sit and have a warm cup of coffee together! It would be great to hear about your church and get to know you and your church's ministry—and, more specifically, to hear how God has placed a burden on your heart for the ministry of the nursery.

If we could sit and talk, I'd ask about your favorite parts of the ministry, and I'd also ask where you feel stuck and need resources to get over the bumps in the road. I'd want to ask how God brought you to the place of serving in the ministry of the nursery and how you see God working in the future. I'd want to brainstorm with you, encourage you in your ministry role, and pray together about it!

This resource is intended to bolster you with practical ideas for the *process* of implementing ministry as well as for the end result. So I'm praying that, as you read this story of how one nursery ministry team formed, you'll be encouraged and motivated to begin (or continue on in) a crucial part of the overall ministry of your church.

Before we continue, let's clarify the use of the word *nursery*. What ages does "nursery" apply to? Churches divide age groups many different ways. In this book, the nursery ministry refers to children three years of age and under. Chapter 7 specifically addresses the issue of different ways your nursery can be divided so that children can best be served in a safe, age-appropriate manner.

In the service of God,
Julia A. Spohrer

ONE

Developing Your Vision

I'm stressed. I'm not sure I can do this, Jackie! I mean, I have no clue what I'm doing. I have two small children, my time is limited, and I just don't know if I can be involved in nursery ministry."

Jackie looked at Claire as they sat at Jackie's kitchen table—Claire's nine-month-old was sleeping in a car seat and her three-year-old was playing on the floor.

"Claire, I know it seems pretty impossible right now. I've been right where you are. I know from experience that it is possible, but you're going to have to be willing to take things one step at a time and truly pray through each step of the process. God wants to use you in this ministry, but he also wants to help you grow in your faith in him. Claire, if you'd like, we could get together again next week and start from the beginning."

"Do you really mean it, Jackie? I need help, and if you could just show me some of the tricks of the trade, well, maybe that would get me back on track."

Jackie and Claire set a time to meet together. They agreed to meet at Claire's church, even though Jackie lived about thirty minutes away in a neighboring town. A woman in her early fifties, Jackie was the coordinator of the nursery ministry at First Church—where she had served for what seemed like a lifetime. She graciously agreed to be Claire's mentor. They didn't ever use the word *mentor* but did agree to meet regularly to connect.

When Claire first called Jackie to set up a visit, she was relieved to hear the warmth in her voice over the phone. Claire had been thinking that if she could talk with someone who had done this before, it could help a little. Claire had no idea Jackie would be willing to connect with her on a regular basis. Claire had found out about Jackie from a friend's mom who had heard about Jackie's incredibly exciting ministry in the nursery at her church. That's what Claire desperately wanted for *her* church—Grace Church. Her pastor talked a lot about reaching people in their community and having great ministries for children, but it seemed that things never got off the ground. He tried hard to cover all the bases, but he was overworked. Claire was the fifth nursery coordinator Pastor Jim had recruited—in about two-and-a-half years. Needless to say, there had been constant turnover in the nursery ministry.

I'm looking forward to getting everything all set in the nursery, Claire thought to herself, forgetting Jackie's caution that she shouldn't think she could whip the nursery ministry into shape in a short time. Claire didn't have a mental picture of what "running like clockwork" meant for nursery ministry, but somehow she was hopeful that it would happen soon. And so she woke up one Sunday morning with extra energy, thinking about serving in her church's nursery ministry.

SUNDAY MORNING AT GRACE CHURCH

Claire had barely gotten out of the car with her children, complete with all their paraphernalia, when her friend's husband greeted her. He wanted to tell her that his kids had become ill during the night, and his wife wouldn't be able to fulfill her nursery responsibilities that morning. Claire tried hard to keep a positive attitude. She smiled, told him she understood, and headed toward the entrance.

That morning Claire ended up missing both her Sunday school class and the worship time because she was putting out fires in the nursery. She went home drained. Her husband, on the other hand, was exuberant after experiencing a great morning of worship and the opportunity to connect with other guys over coffee and donuts. Doubts flashed through her mind again about serving in this ministry. The stress was definitely more than she had bargained for. Now, more than ever, she was looking forward to meeting with Jackie in the coming week. *I can only hope*, thought Claire, *that she'll help me know what to do.*

VISION VISIT

Claire and Jackie met in the nursery at Claire's church. The children played contentedly while Claire and Jackie sat in the only two chairs in the room—rocking chairs. "So, Claire, what's on your mind today with the nursery ministry?"

"I'm still not sure I can do this, Jackie. I didn't get to go to worship again on Sunday, and I'm feeling overwhelmed. Why is this job so difficult? And why is it so hard to get people to help?"

Jackie paused for a moment. She had a calm spirit about her.

"Claire, what you're feeling and experiencing is a normal part of the process of learning about this ministry. I know it may sound odd, but it's true. I have dozens of pages in my journal that reflect my frustrations when I first started out in this ministry area. I actually wrote down my conversations with God—partly because I was feeling so helpless and partly because my husband got tired of me complaining. So I started complaining on paper. It turned out to be my way of crying out to God for help."

While Jackie was talking, Claire was thinking, *She's not giving me much to go on here.* Claire knew that Jackie was trying to be encouraging, but she wanted straightforward and practical answers—a list of what to do and what not to do to fix everything that was wrong.

Jackie must have been reading Claire's mind, because she switched gears. "Claire, where do you think 'starting at the beginning' means we'll start?"

"It seems like it all starts with recruiting."

Jackie nodded. "That's true, recruiting is very important. I think, though, we need to start with the big picture before we talk about anything else."

"What do you mean by 'big picture'?"

"Well, before we jump into details such as recruiting problems and figuring out what supplies are needed, we have to look at how you picture the nursery ministry functioning when it's fixed."

This idea of conceptualizing the end product was perplexing to Claire, who wasn't grasping what Jackie was trying to say. All Claire knew was that she wanted the nursery to run smoothly—and that she had no idea what to do to make that happen.

IMAGINE WHAT YOUR NURSERY COULD BE

Jackie shared her big-picture vision with Claire. "Imagine that your church has the nursery that everyone in town wants to come and see! There's a buzz, and it's not just in your church—it's spreading from neighborhood to neighborhood. The word is out in your community. Everyone has heard that babies are welcomed tenderly at your church and parents are comforted by how fine-tuned the nursery ministry is. There are more than enough loving adults waiting to rock and read to the babies, and moms and dads feel confident knowing that while they're at worship or in Sunday school, their children's needs will be met. In fact, nursery workers are so excited about the opportunity to minister to the church's youngest people that they take pictures of the children so they can pray for each child throughout the week.

"Imagine that when parents return to pick up their child, they pause in amazement as they see a most wonderful sight— a young couple (part of the nursery team) kneeling by their child and praying God's blessings for him or her. As they walk into the room, they are greeted warmly by nursery workers. It's fun for the parents to hear the animated stories of what went on in the nursery as they hear their child mentioned by name— just another reminder that their child is being well cared for and nurtured in this place.

"Imagine that the warmth of your nursery workers fits in perfectly with the bright, clean, cheerful decor of the rooms dedicated for the care of these precious children. It is obvious to all who walk by—even those who see from a distance—that the room was carefully designed and is now deliberately maintained to be age-appropriate and user-friendly for all who come into contact with this ministry.

"Imagine that the word is out in the mom network that your church's nursery even cares about the spread of germs and has policies in place to prevent the infamous spread of sicknesses that often originate in church nurseries. Imagine that even the dads in your town are talking. Yes, even the dad network is bubbling with news about your nursery! The dads are talking because they notice the men who are a part of the staff team in the nursery ministry. Dads of teenagers, granddads, and friends of dads are volunteering their time to be involved with the children—to get on the floor and build towers with blocks and sit in rocking chairs to look at pictures in a book."

"Okay, okay," Claire said, breaking into Jackie's monologue. "I'm hooked! *That's* what I want to see happen at Grace Church—what you just said! So how do I get there?"

Jackie looked intently at her and said, "Claire, what I've just been describing is my *vision* for the nursery ministry. Even after years and years as coordinator, everything isn't always picture-perfect. What keeps my team and me going is that we keep reminding each other and our congregation of our vision for the nursery ministry. I believe God has given our nursery team this vision for the benefit of our church's overall ministry."

"How did you get this vision," Claire asked, "and how do you make it happen?"

With a big smile, Jackie responded, "Claire, I'm really glad you asked. I've jotted down some notes for you. I've been going back through the notes, books, and other resources I've used over the years. I thought it may be helpful to put some things in writing."

Right about then Claire's youngest was finding her voice, letting Claire know that the talk was coming to an end. Jackie helped Claire straighten up the room and pack up their belongings. As they walked to the parking lot, Jackie handed Claire a notebook. "I'll call you in a week or two to find out how things are going," said Jackie as they went their separate ways.

JACKIE'S NOTES

Later that evening, Claire picked up the notebook and turned to Jackie's notes:

PREPARE FOR THE MINISTRY

Step 1: Develop your vision.

Step 2: Gather a team.

Step 3: Evaluate and set goals.

These steps are sometimes easy to skip — especially if you've just been asked to be in charge of the nursery ministry. We want to get to the good stuff and have the room set up beautifully, have the nursery workers recruited, and have all the policies in place.

Here's what can happen when the person in charge skips the first three steps of ministry:

✓ One person (or just a few people) can end up doing all the work.

✓ The in-charge person (or persons) can get excited and motivated at the beginning, but in time they can begin to feel isolated and to think that no one else in the church has an interest in the ministry.

✓ The in-charge person (or persons) can get resentful, feeling that if they don't do everything, no one else will.

✓ The in-charge person (or persons) can burn out, leaving a gap in the ministry until the next person steps forward to do the ministry.

✓ It can be difficult for the next person to carry on the ministry because the vision and goals haven't been put in writing.

Here's what can happen when you patiently follow the first three steps of the ministry:

- ✓ The ministry dreams (vision) and goals are discussed and put in writing (providing motivation to continue rather than burn out).
- ✓ A ministry team is established (no lone rangers).
- ✓ The evaluation process allows for the team to celebrate when dreams and goals are accomplished (you can see where you've been and where you are headed).
- ✓ Over time, your ministry dreams become a reality!

DO THE WORK OF THE MINISTRY

Step 4: Set up the nursery environment.

Step 5: Develop policies and procedures for your ministry.

Step 6: Recruit the people you need to staff your nursery.

Step 7: Establish an understanding of what children can learn at each level.

These are the four steps during which you and your team will begin to see the vision for your nursery ministry become reality!

A LITTLE MORE ADVICE ON VISION

Let's start at the beginning with your dreams for your church's nursery ministry by looking at step 1.

Take a moment to write out your dreams for this ministry. You may want to designate a particular notebook to record your vision. The vision worksheet below can serve as a guide to inform your thinking.

Vision Worksheet

❑ What do you want children and parents to experience when they come into contact with this ministry? What kind of experience do you want babies and toddlers to have? What do you want parents to feel when they drop off their children? What do you want parents to think as they consider the impact of this ministry area?

I imagine a time when our nursery . . .

❑ What kind of reputation in your church and community do you want your nursery to have, and how will this specific ministry impact the overall ministry of your church?

I imagine a time when our nursery . . .

❑ What do you want your nursery environment to look like? What experience do you want babies and toddlers to have in this environment? How do you want people to feel when they walk into the room or look inside as they walk by?

I imagine a time when our nursery . . .

❑ What are the policies you believe you need in order for your nursery to run smoothly? What information do you want parents and nursery workers to know? What is the role of communication as it relates to your nursery ministry?

I imagine a time when our nursery . . .

Reasons to Keep Your Completed Vision Worksheet

❑ You will want to refer to this worksheet and add ideas and dreams as you keep moving through this evaluation process.

❑ Having your vision in writing will help you as you communicate with your church leaders and members. A written vision document can be a great tool as you share your excitement and seek to motivate others to be a part of this important ministry.

❑ You can encourage parents of young children by letting them know that this ministry is important and that it is developing with the best interests of their children in mind.

A Little More Advice on Vision

The idea of vision has become increasingly promoted in church leadership books. Many churches and organizations are developing vision statements—which is a great thing to do. However, developing a statement that tries to capture a living, dynamic, powerful vision is not only difficult, it is *not enough* all by itself. The vision worksheet can guide your thinking as you ask God to give you a picture of the ministry's fullest potential. If you can work with a team and turn these thoughts into a statement, that's great! Just don't forget that the statement (or even the completed vision worksheets) won't help you at all unless you are continually—and I mean seeing that it's peppered through *every conversation*—communicating this vision!

It may take months to fully develop the vision for your particular ministry. So continue to take notes and work on developing your vision, but don't hesitate to tackle the next steps as you're refining the vision for the ministry. Pray for patience and wisdom, and keep writing down the ideas God gives you. Be sure to keep talking about the vision with the people who will be added to your team.

QUESTIONS FOR REFLECTION AND DISCUSSION

1. Describe your church's current nursery ministry. What kind of reputation does it have in your church? What is your role in it? What do you find most rewarding about your church's nursery ministry?

2. Take some time to work through the vision worksheet in this chapter. Share your ideas and dreams with at least one other person in your church.

TWO

Gathering Your Team

Claire was busy with family responsibilities and couldn't get together with Jackie for a couple of weeks. But they did manage to carve out about twenty minutes on the phone one afternoon. Claire shared with Jackie her appreciation for the notes Jackie had put together for her.

Jackie seemed pleased that Claire was able to use what she had been given. "Now we need to pray, Claire, that God sends you a partner or two for this ministry." She went on to explain a few things. (Claire took notes on a paper towel and later transferred this practical advice to her now growing file of notes from Jackie.) Here's the gist of what Jackie told Claire:

DON'T BE A LONE RANGER

✓ Pray for a partner (or two or three) with whom you can share your heart and vision for this ministry.

✓ Pray that God brings to your mind names of people to ask to consider partnering with you in ministry.

✓ Let the person (or persons) know you are looking for someone to pray with, to brainstorm with, and to take ownership with you in the ministry.

✓ Let the person (or persons) hear your excitement about the potential and about your need for their help (along with others) in reaching this potential.

✓ Communicate that this is a practical step you're taking in forming a team to make this ministry happen.

Before Claire and Jackie finished their phone conversation, Claire was a bit surprised to hear Jackie mention a few names and telephone numbers. "Claire, I know you don't have a lot of extra time on your hands, but give these three women a call. I'll call them today and let them know you'll be calling. Don't just take *my* word for it—ask them about the time I asked them to partner with me in ministry. Maybe hearing from them will help you as you think and pray through this next step in the process."

LESSONS FROM JACKIE'S TEAM MEMBERS

As she talked to the women Jackie had asked to join the team when she began her nursery ministry, Claire discovered that Jackie took the time to genuinely connect with people. She didn't make a hurried or panicked plea for help. It became clear that what the women remembered was the enthusiasm, passion, and vision Jackie had for the ministry. Claire began to understand more clearly why the vision for the ministry is so important. As a result of what she heard from Brigit, Anne, and Elise, she resolved to continue praying for one or two partners in ministry.

Brigit

"Yes, I remember when Jackie first asked me about working with her to get the nursery ministry going. I had no idea what I was getting into. Wow, it is so incredible to see what great things God has done since then! What was it about our conversation that made me want to get involved? I remember sensing that Jackie had a big smile on her face as we talked. Even though I couldn't see her face, I could just tell she was envisioning an incredible ministry with the nursery at our church. To be honest, I was skeptical about what could be so great about a nursery, but I could sense her conviction that taking good care of our church family's littlest people was a critically important ministry. She described how she saw the ministry developing and what her ideal picture—her vision—was, and she said she could picture me being a vital part of making it happen."

Anne

"Jackie told me she wanted me to pray about being a part of a small team to work in this ministry area. I told her I wasn't very excited about changing diapers and being involved in the "caring for babies" stage. But she said there was much more to this ministry, and then she described her ultimate dreams for the ministry—her vision. She said she had a particular role in mind for me. She had observed my gifts of encouragement and shepherding. Though I didn't understand the specifics at the time, she envisioned me as the one who could make reminder calls and encourage the team of people working in our nursery on Sunday mornings."

Elise

"Jackie and I and our kids met at the play area at McDonalds. Our kids played together while Jackie and I indulged in ice cream sundaes. She shared with me her passion for the nursery ministry and a picture—a vision—of the potential she saw. I had never heard anyone so energized about a ministry—and so convicted about its importance for both children as well as parents. Just hearing about the opportunity to serve God in this way, I wanted in."

MAKING THE CALLS

Claire prayed specifically about asking three women to partner with her in this ministry. She was nervous about asking, because she wanted to do a good job of sharing the vision for the nursery—just as Jackie had done in her conversations with Brigit, Anne, and Elise—but it was something new for her. She called her best friend and asked her to pray, and then she picked up the phone while the children were napping.

It took Claire about a week to finally connect with all three of the women she'd been praying about calling. After talking at length with each of them, she was thrilled when Kate agreed to join in this ministry. Claire called Jackie to let her know the good news. After expressing her excitement, Jackie surprised Claire with her next question: "How about if you, Kate, and I get together soon. We'll walk through one or two more steps, and we can pray together, too!"

"Jackie, that sounds wonderful. I'm so thankful that God brought you into my life. You are helping me so much."

QUESTIONS FOR REFLECTION AND DISCUSSION

1. What are the benefits of working with a partner or team in ministry?

2. What (if anything) is preventing you from working with a partner in ministry?

THREE

Evaluating and Setting Goals

Claire and Kate, her new partner in ministry, arranged for a baby-sitter to care for their children and met Jackie at a local diner. On the way, Claire and Kate talked about a conversation they'd been having with a parent of one of the children in the nursery. This parent had been expressing her concern that their church needed new carpet in the room and more toys for the children. She also thought they needed a better system for making sure that the toys were cleaned on a regular basis. Even though Claire and Kate knew the parent was right, hearing these expressions of concern felt draining. They agreed to ask Jackie how they should respond.

Jackie was sitting at a table in the corner of the diner. She threw her arms around Kate as though she were a long lost child. "Kate, you are an answer to prayer, you know. It's so nice to meet you."

The three of them chatted awhile, and then Claire and Kate began sharing what they'd been discussing in the car. Jackie listened intently—interested in hearing all the details. When they asked her what to do, she asked, "Well, what do *you* think you should do?"

Claire and Kate looked at each other. Kate said, "I know this mom is right about some things that need to be done, but frankly, Jackie, I'm so new at this, and it seems as though there are so many different areas that need to be addressed."

There was a pause, and then Claire added, "Jackie, I'm still somewhat overwhelmed. Part of the vision I've been developing is to have a bright and clean nursery with age-appropriate toys, along with a great system for making sure the toys are clean. But there are also a *lot* of other things on my vision worksheet—and they're all begging for my attention at the same time! I don't know how it can all get done."

JACKIE'S ADVICE

Claire and Kate cradled their coffee cups in their hands as they listened to Jackie share her perspective on a practical, realistic approach to ministry. Jackie encouraged them to take time to listen to people's ideas—to truly listen without immediately assuming that they had to implement all the ideas. Claire couldn't help but think, *How refreshing not to think we have to do it all!* Jackie pointed them back to the team approach, reminding them that the more they listened and gathered ideas, the more contagious the excitement would become and the more people would be drawn to be a part of the ministry.

Jackie was right. Armed with this commitment to listen and gather ideas, Claire and Kate were able to resist the temptation to promise people that they would implement all their great ideas right away. Instead they shared their vision for the ministry and told them they were simply collecting ideas to help set goals for the coming year to reach what they envisioned for the ministry.

Because Jackie had encouraged Claire and Kate to invite people to the team who realistically had the time to devote to the development of the ministry, they intentionally asked people to pray about whether they'd have the time to invest to help implement some of the goals being crafted throughout this listening stage.

Jackie was a methodical person who loved to create lists. Yet, as Claire and Kate met with her that day, Jackie was very intentional about reminding them that the ministry process *cannot* be reduced only to lists. The lists were merely guides to help get them started. Jackie warned them of the danger of getting sidetracked by relying on her lists and her ideas rather than on their process of listening to people's ideas, gathering and working with a team, and continually seeking God in prayer about the direction of the ministry and the next steps to take.

Now having said this, Jackie did pass on a helpful list of steps to take for evaluating the ministry and for setting goals.

STEPS FOR EVALUATION AND GOAL SETTING

1. Build momentum and ownership by asking questions.
   ✓ Ask current nursery workers to share their ideas for improving the ministry. Have them fill out an evaluation survey (see sample in appendix 5).
   ✓ Ask parents to give you their feedback on the ministry.
   ✓ Let people know you are collecting ideas for the goal-setting process so that you can take the ministry to the next level; make sure they know that their feedback is important.

2. Pray for God's guidance in the evaluation process.
   ✓ As you collect and compile the information, make lists of people's ideas, concerns, and feedback.
   ✓ Pray for wisdom and a spirit of openness in understanding others' perspectives.

3. Set goals.
   ✓ Make a master list of all ideas and issues that need to be addressed.
   ✓ Have each person on the team write down the three or four items that are most important to him or her.
   ✓ Have everyone share what they wrote down, and record these priorities on the master list.
   ✓ As a team look at the group's response. Continue to work as a group to narrow down the list.
   ✓ As a group agree on the top three priorities to establish as goals for the next year.

4. Communicate the goals.
   ✓ Make sure the goals are clearly stated and recorded.
   ✓ Incorporate the goals into church newsletter articles, notes to parents, notes to staff members, and into your conversations with church members.
   ✓ Build excitement by letting people know specifically what the team is working toward in the ministry. Let people know the context of the goals; remind them that the goals are steps to living out the vision. Communicating the goals allows another opportunity to share the vision of where the ministry is going.

5. Divide and conquer.
   ✓ Write down each step to be taken in order to accomplish each goal.
   ✓ Assign a person (or persons) to oversee the progress of each goal.

✓ Write down the parts of the process of accomplishing the goals that could be delegated to parents and to staff members within the ministry.

6. Don't be afraid to ask.
   ✓ Ask many people to take part in the process.
   ✓ The more people who have a job to do — big or little — the more ownership there will be in the ministry.

7. Communicate progress.
   ✓ Establish a key communication person to give regular updates on the progress of the goals. Let people know when parts of a goal have been accomplished.
   ✓ Inform people of the steps taken along the way in reaching the goals. Doing so will allow them to keep learning about and gaining an appreciation for the ministry.
   ✓ Publicly thank people who have been a part of reaching the goals. Doing so will show that it has been a team effort involving many people working together to reach the goal.

QUESTIONS FOR REFLECTION AND DISCUSSION

1. What are some ways to respond to parents who come to you with suggestions for additional furnishings and equipment in the church nursery?

2. As you look through the steps for evaluation and goal setting provided in this chapter, what are the next steps your church nursery ministry could be taking? Who should be involved, and when should you begin?

FOUR

Setting Up the Nursery Environment

Several days later Jackie contacted Claire and told her about an upcoming workshop on nursery ministry. The workshop was to take place at a church a couple of hours away, and Jackie was speaking on some of the same issues they'd been discussing. Jackie invited Claire to ride with her to the workshop.

The day came, and Claire sat and listened to Jackie give her presentation at the workshop. Throughout the course of Jackie's talk, Claire jotted down observations in her notebook:

THE NURSERY ENVIRONMENT

People often ask the question, "What do I need for our nursery?" They're usually looking for a specific list. They ask whether to have shelves to hold diaper bags, or if it's better to have hooks on the walls to hang them on. They ask how many rocking chairs they need, and whether or not they should have cribs or just use car seats or bouncy seats or infant swings.

In the ideal world, it would be great to have the nursery completely furnished — and updated — every year. It would be great to have the perfect amount of space and the best location within the church building. But it's also important to balance vision with reality. It doesn't mean you should stop picturing the ideal of how you see God working in this ministry. But it does mean being willing to wait on God's timing — which may be different from yours. Every church is different. The physical environment of the ministry is an important part of the vision, but it's not the only piece. Since it's such a tangible part of the ministry, it's easy to get myopic and neglect other aspects of the vision.

Perhaps having a sink and running water in your church nursery isn't possible right now. The danger is to get so focused on accomplishing the recommendations on a list that the main purpose gets overshadowed — which is to minister God's love to children and their parents.

As you think about your nursery's environment, consider these recommendations for equipment and supplies:

Equipment and Furniture

Item	Recommended Number
Rocking chair	1 per 2 babies
Changing table	1 per 8 babies/toddlers
Sink	1 per room
Refrigerator	1 per nursery area
Swing	1 per 3 babies
Exersaucer	1 per 8 babies
Check-in area	1 per room

Supply List

Toys

Towels

Disinfectant

Hooks or cubbies for diaper bags

Gloves

Vacuum and broom

Extra diapers

Cheerios for snacks (for toddlers)

Blankets

*Powder Dam
Extra set of clothing
Cloth diapers for burping cloths

*Powder Dam is a powdered gel absorbent — a must-have for ministries with children. If a child gets sick and doesn't make it to the rest room, sprinkle the powder on the affected area of the carpet, and any liquid will be absorbed. Follow up by vacuuming. To order call 1-800-782-2436.

Some steps to take in evaluating your nursery's environment and what to do about it:

1. Investigate the history of your nursery. Who were the previous decision makers? What was their particular course of action, and why did they choose it? Ask someone on your team to find out the answers to these and other questions you may have and then report back to the team. This information will help you move forward with consideration and respect for others who have worked hard before you, with new sources of wisdom, and with the ability to see (and hopefully better understand) the process that has led the church to this point.
2. Make a list of what's great about your nursery right now — before anything is updated or changed.
3. Honestly evaluate your nursery's needs.

<u>Why</u>, you may wonder, <u>should I take the time to make a list of what's great about my nursery now when I know it needs improvement in the future?</u> Throughout the

evaluation process, it's important not to be overcome with a negative spirit. It can be discouraging sometimes to see how far we are from our ideal. But it's important to continue on with the process, no matter how overwhelming it feels, because doing so will build a strong foundation for your nursery ministry. Having a negative spirit and focusing on everything that needs to be changed will only make it more difficult to be encouraging and to be an active part of the solution.

For example, if you have a negative cloud around you and you hear that the new carpet can't be installed until a year from now, you'll probably struggle to stay positive and focused. If you take time to make a list of what's working in your ministry and concentrate on keeping the positive aspects going well, it'll be easier to wait for improvements to be made. When you refrain from looking at everything through a negative lens, you'll be able to be a creative problem solver.

Sometimes momentum for ministry stalls at the churchwide decision-making process. People don't always agree on how church decisions should be made. Some think it should take less time; some think a certain process is the only way. Churches go through changes in how they make decisions, too, so you may have an opportunity in the future to suggest changes and updates for your particular ministry. There is an appropriate time to do so. It's important, however, not to confuse the issues of getting resources for the nursery and changing how the church makes decisions. If you'd like to have more resources allocated to the nursery ministry, then respect and follow your church's current process and procedures. Even if you are frustrated by this process, it's the one that is available to you to move ahead with your vision and your team's vision for what God is doing in the ministry. So don't get distracted by the process. Let the process work for you and the team, and keep your focus on God's work in the ministry.

It will be important to communicate with parents and your nursery staff members how the process works. Here's a sample letter:

Dear parents and nursery staff,

We are excited about our dream of adding some new resources for our nursery ministry in the next year. Our wish list includes: installation of new carpet, a mini-refrigerator, and one additional rocking chair. We've submitted a budget proposal that would allow us to purchase these items. As the process continues, we'll keep you updated. We may need to wait to add the mini-refrigerator because we will need additional wiring. While it may seem to be a simple problem to solve, apparently there are major electrical repairs that need to be done in our church building. It may make more sense to have these issues addressed all at one time, which may be a year from now.

We continue to be thankful that God has brought new families with young children to our community and to our church family. It's exciting to see our nursery staff doing such a great job in caring for the children. Parents, the next time you drop off your child in the nursery, take a moment to let the nursery staff people know that you appreciate their commitment to serving in this ministry.

Serving the Lord, and thankful for YOU,
The Nursery Ministry Team

A PASTOR'S PERSPECTIVE

Jackie and Claire sat together at the workshop's final session. The pastor of the sponsoring church shared his perspective, which Claire found to be particularly helpful:

"Last year a few people got excited about renovating a space for children's church. They came to me one day with a list of great ideas to make the space more inviting and more effective for ministry to children in age-appropriate ways. They wanted permission to begin implementing their ideas within the next month. When I mentioned that our budget and planning process took longer than a month to sign off on their desired changes, they accused me of being unsupportive of the children's ministry and of not valuing the children.

"About two months later, the nursery ministry team came and asked a lot of questions. They asked how the planning and budgeting process worked. They asked how they could better support the vision of the church as a whole within the nursery ministry. They asked how they could pray for me and shared their excitement about the church. They told me a story about how a family had recently rededicated their lives to Christ. One of the key moments in their journey was experiencing a warm welcome when they visited our church and when they took their youngest child to the nursery. The nursery team was thrilled at how God used them in ministering to this couple. I was so encouraged by this story. In fact, the whole experience with the nursery team was positive.

"They made a budget proposal and gave it to the finance committee, carefully following the process I had described. Periodically, one of the team members would send an e-mail message and fill me in on the progress of their proposals. I felt energized by them and motivated to help them succeed. It was as though we had a mutual trust and a commitment to encouragement. I'm confident that this team is loyal to the church and will work for the church's unity. I think they're confident that I'm truly grateful for them and that I value their ministry."

TO HAVE A CRIB, OR NOT TO HAVE A CRIB

On the way home, Jackie and Claire talked about the crib dilemma. Claire had always thought that a nursery had to have cribs. Jackie helped her look at the dilemma in a new way. She told Claire about the two reasons to have cribs in a church nursery—the first, of course, is to have a place for babies to sleep, and the second, and less obvious, reason is to have a safe means of emergency exit in case of fire or other evacuation emergency (provided that the crib has wheels, like hospital cribs do).

Having a hospital-type crib wasn't an option for Jackie's church. They found that most infants (those most likely to sleep in the nursery) were brought in a car seat or carrier of some sort. In the case of an emergency, the car seat or carrier can be used to exit the nursery. Jackie's church decided, therefore, at least in part because of space limitations, to have one port-a-crib and not purchase regular cribs with wheels.

In using car seats and carriers on a regular basis, they learned some things the hard way—first, that they needed to *label* the seats, just as they did with diaper bags, and second (and most important), that they needed to *communicate* with parents regarding the child's safety. For example, it wasn't unusual for nursery workers to leave the safety belt unattached on a child sleeping in a car seat. It would happen on occasion, then, that the parents would pick up the child from the nursery, not notice that the belt wasn't attached, and place the child in the car and drive home. Communication can prevent this type of situation from resulting in a surprised and upset set of parents upon their arrival home.

Jackie summed up her thoughts this way: "Don't be afraid, Claire, to think of different ways of accomplishing the same goal. And when you do try a different way, expect that your team will learn from experience and make adjustments as appropriate. They'll be able to say, 'This is what we learned,' and they'll continue to have ownership in the ministry."

Claire appreciated the time she spent with Jackie in the car. As they got closer to home, Claire told Jackie about how much her team had grown—with four people now on the nursery ministry team. Jackie had been right. In the process of sharing the vision and listening and getting input from parents and staff members in the evaluation and goal-setting process, Claire had added two new members to the team. Claire asked Jackie to come to her next nursery team meeting to share ideas on how to become better organized and how to set up effective policies and procedures.

QUESTIONS FOR REFLECTION AND DISCUSSION

1. What do you think is great about your nursery right now? What is currently working well?

2. How does your church make decisions? How are budget proposals prepared and submitted? What are some of your current nursery ministry's needs that you and your team agree require additional resources? What should you be doing as a result of these needs?

3. What are some equipment needs you think your nursery has at present? How would you go about building a good case for your church to respond to these needs?

FIVE

Developing Policies and Procedures

Jackie came to Claire's nursery team meeting a few weeks later. Claire met her in the entrance of the church, and they walked to the classroom together.

"Claire," said Jackie, "I know you'd like me to talk about policies and procedures and how to organize your team, and I'm happy to do that, but I'd also like to model another way of holding a workshop. I'm praying that you'll watch the process we go through and that you'll notice the environment and interaction. The next time you and I get together, I'd love to look at the issue of recruiting and help you prepare to lead a discussion with your team on this area of ministry. You may want to incorporate in that meeting some of the same methods and dynamics you'll observe today in the discussion on policies and procedures and organizing your ministry. Are you up for this challenge, Claire?"

"I appreciate your encouragement, Jackie, and the fact that you believe in me. I'll be watching and listening extra carefully today. I'm glad you're sharing this idea before the meeting, so I can learn from you—and I look forward to your help in getting ready for the next meeting."

CAUGHT OFF GUARD, YET EXCITED BY THE CHALLENGE

While in one sense Claire was caught off guard by Jackie's challenge, on the other hand she was excited that Jackie truly believed in her. Claire felt energized and increasingly excited about this ministry God had laid on her heart. This was progress, for these thoughts and feelings were much different from when she had first met with Jackie. God was truly at work in Claire's life, using Jackie to encourage her to trust him each step of the way in this ministry—not that the ministry was easy, but Claire could sense that she had grown, and this reality alone was encouraging.

Jackie opened the meeting with a heartfelt prayer for all of them to be focused on ministering to young children and their families. Then she got out an easel and flip chart and began asking questions. She would ask a question about a particular area, and then the nursery team would create lists (Jackie recorded the ideas on the flip chart for all to see). This approach surprised Claire. She had thought Jackie was going to teach them—that she'd come in and tell them how to organize their ministry and what their policies and procedures should be.

The group took a break after forty-five minutes, and Claire pulled Jackie aside to ask a question: "Why are you asking us questions and having us make these lists instead of just telling us how you do your policies and procedures at your church?"

Jackie smiled and said, "I love it that you're asking me this question. There are a couple of reasons I'm doing it this way. I'll answer your question, but I'd like to answer it while your other team members can interact with this question as well."

So after the break, Jackie was back by the easel with a new color marker, and she was ready to answer Claire's question. She asked the group to think about why they were thinking, brainstorming, and making lists together when she could simply share the way her church set up their nursery. After thinking about it and discussing it for a few moments, these are some of the answers that began to flow:

- ❑ It helps us to think carefully about the issue or subject rather than just be told this is the way it is. We're recognizing that there's more than one way to accomplish a certain aspect of the ministry.
- ❑ We have the opportunity to hear and understand each other's perspectives.
- ❑ It helps us as a team to have a collective sense of ownership. We're examining the issues together and simultaneously developing a plan.
- ❑ Even though you don't "tell us" a certain way, you do incorporate principles of interaction you've come to see as essential to the ministry.
- ❑ We have the opportunity to tweak ideas to fit the atmosphere and nuances of our church family. We don't have to go back and do that now, because you're giving us the opportunity to interact as we go through this process.

Jackie was beaming. "Yes, yes, you've got it! Your team is headed for some incredible times of ministry together. This is great! Okay, now with all this in mind, let's get back to work and finish up by 11:30." Everyone in the group took notes, and Claire later arranged these into this summary about policies and procedures:

POLICIES AND PROCEDURES

✓ Policies and procedures are the <u>written guidelines</u> that serve as part of the foundation for the ministry. They allow participants (both parents and nursery workers) to know what is expected, no matter what your role on the team might be.

✓ Policies and procedures are crucial for effective nursery ministry. If they don't function at the foundation of your ministry, everyone will do what's right in their own eyes (see Judges 17:6), which will produce a sense of unsettledness in the ministry. When you have them in place, there is a sense of consistency and stability. People understand what is expected.

✓ Parents generally understand that children function best where there are clear boundaries. The church has a great opportunity to support parents in establishing these boundaries by creating and implementing clear policies and procedures in the nursery ministry environment.

✓ Nursery ministry policies and procedures are intended to help both nursery workers and parents. Nursery workers must understand what their job is in caring for the children. They have to understand when they are expected to be in the nursery and what to do if they can't be there at the expected time. They need to be informed about how to handle emergencies and how to welcome new parents. Finally, they must understand what is expected of parents who bring their children to the nursery.

✓ Parents need a clear understanding of what they're supposed to do at the time they drop off their children. They should know whether they are expected to serve in the nursery, and they should understand what is expected of the nursery caregivers — which will help parents feel more secure about leaving their children.

✓ Policies and procedures should be visibly displayed so everyone knows what they are. For example, if you have a diaper-changing policy, it's important to have these expectations clearly written out and displayed near the diaper-changing station. Keep in mind, though, that the mere presence of signs in your nursery doesn't necessarily mean that you've adequately communicated your policies and procedures.

IMPLEMENTING POLICIES AND PROCEDURES

There are two approaches to implementing policies and procedures — the <u>responsive</u> approach and the <u>proactive</u> approach. While it is great to be proactive, at times the responsive approach is preferred. Both have their place in the various times and seasons of ministry. Remember, too, that policies and procedures may have once been formulated but haven't been communicated in a long time. In these cases people may not even know there are policies and procedures; and even if they do recall them, they may not have a sense of ownership.

The <u>responsive approach</u> is required when you begin to notice a pattern of feedback on a particular topic. As you do, you begin to ask yourself whether it's time to implement a new policy or procedure. For example, you notice a pattern among the teenagers who've been asked to serve in the nursery. They are starting to bring their friends, and the teens are just hanging out instead of paying attention to the needs of the children. You begin to get a few phone calls from nursery workers, alerting you to this concern. It may well be time to work on creating and implementing a policy to ensure that excessive numbers of people aren't hanging out in the nursery in a way that deflects attention from the safety and nurture of children.

In the <u>proactive approach</u>, you brainstorm ideas and you think ahead — you focus on prevention, so to speak. Policies and procedures proactively implemented in a ministry often "solve" problems before they even occur.

- ✓ With your team, make a list of policies and procedures you think you'd like to implement.
- ✓ Prioritize the list.
- ✓ Pick three to five items to work on first.
- ✓ Check out options (see what other churches have done).
- ✓ Tweak any policies and procedures you've gleaned from other churches to make them your own.
- ✓ Make sure you communicate the policies.

COMMUNICATING POLICIES AND PROCEDURES

Take great care to communicate to all who need to know. Teams often do a great job in patiently and carefully developing the necessary policies and procedures. A problem arises, however, when they talk with a parent or nursery caregiver who hasn't had the benefit of all the thinking that's gone into the new policy or procedure —

and the parent or nursery worker raises several questions that may have been answered if a communication plan had been followed. Good policies and procedures are often short-circuited because parents or nursery workers feel that the policy developers haven't communicated well or gotten enough input from them. When a team develops new policies, it's wise to think of the process in three steps.

1. Develop a draft.
2. Share the draft with the people involved in the ministry.
3. Collect input and ideas to incorporate into the final draft, and be sure to communicate the starting date of implementation.

It can be challenging to be patient as you develop and implement policies. While not every single person has to sign off on every single policy or procedure, the process of getting input gives people time to process change. When people have this time, they're more likely to embrace the policy or procedure; without this time, the implementation often quickly fizzles because people haven't embraced the ideas.

Here are some things to do after collaboration and before implementation:

✓ Communicate in writing two to four weeks before implementation.
✓ Verbally communicate with those who are directly affected. For example, if you are implementing a new check-in/drop-off system, you may want to have

a phone-calling party with team members to call all
parents and nursery workers involved.
✓ Communicate with church staff members, ministry
leaders, and elders to keep them informed.
✓ Communicate in writing — using letters, e-mail
messages, and newsletters.

Sample parent letter from Jackie's church regarding
policies and procedures:

Dear parents,

Welcome to our nursery at First Church. We
consider it a privilege to serve your young child
through our nursery ministry! It is our desire to create
a safe and nurturing atmosphere for your child. We
also desire to keep the communication lines open
between you as parents and our church family — and
specifically our nursery ministry.

The following are the policy guidelines we've
established as part of our nursery ministry. We
appreciate you taking time to read and comply with
them. We also appreciate knowing that you will
communicate your feedback and ideas to us as we
continue to grow and change in our ministry.

1. Each child should be signed in by a parent when
   brought to the nursery. We would like parents to
   complete an information card for each child. This
   card will remain in the nursery; it only needs to be
   filled out once and updated if necessary.
2. Parents are requested to label bottles, diaper bags,
   etc., with the child's name.

3. Parents will be given a numbered tag. Fill out the check-in sheet on the counter; be sure to jot down the number in the appropriate space. Return the tag when you pick up your child.

4. If a parent arrives before the caregivers, the parent is requested to stay with the child. Children should not be left alone. If at all possible, the same parent should drop off and pick up the child. Please do not send older children to drop off or pick up the child. If an adult other than a parent has permission from the parent to pick up the child, please notify the nursery caregiver(s) in advance.

5. Parents are requested to pick up their child as soon as possible at the close of each church activity.

6. Caregivers are not permitted to give medication to any child.

7. Parents are requested to notify the nursery caregivers of any allergies or special instructions or needs with regard to their child. Allergy information and special instructions should also be included on the check-in sheet each time your child is in attendance.

8. Children showing any sign of illness or having a fever, a cold, or any contagious disease should not be in the nursery (coughing, runny nose, labored breathing, fever, etc.).

9. After children have their second birthday, they can move up to the two-year-old class.

10. Parents are invited to discuss possible improvements with any of the nursery ministry team members.

Jackie also shared with Claire's team a policy she's seen other churches implement: "All nursery workers must remove their shoes before entering behind the welcome counter. All workers must put on a set of surgical slippers over their socks, nylons, or bare feet. This will keep the carpet clean for infants and crawlers. It will also prevent stepping on little fingers and toes with hard shoes." Jackie's team had decided not to implement this policy, and Claire's team agreed that it wasn't necessary for their nursery at present. However, they decided to file the idea in the notebook, along with their vision worksheets and evaluation and goal-setting notes. If needed in the future, they'd have the idea readily available for discussion and possible implementation.

THE KINDS OF JOBS IN NURSERY MINISTRY

The last part of the nursery team session with Jackie was devoted to a discussion about how to organize as a ministry team in order to be most effective and productive. Jackie continued to guide them as they walked through the various issues she raised.

The team identified a number of different kinds of jobs needed in order to carry out a great nursery ministry:

❑ nursery caregiving
❑ cleaning (see nursery cleaning list in appendix 10)
❑ recruiting, scheduling, and shepherding nursery caregivers
❑ developing policy drafts and overseeing communication of policies and procedures

❏ contributing articles to church newsletters and bulletins
❏ purchasing supplies

Jackie encouraged them to keep developing this list as a team, and then to divide up the responsibilities among team members, as well as invite other people to get involved in taking responsibility for items on the list.

DELEGATING

Jackie shared from her heart the things she had learned about delegating: "I've found that people are often very willing to get involved. It's interesting, because for several years I had been pretty discouraged, thinking that no one wanted to help and become involved. In reality, though, I found that people weren't getting involved because I wasn't taking the time to describe exactly what had to be done."

So Jackie did something about it. "I've learned," Jackie explained to Claire's team, "that if our nursery team sees a job that's integral to the ministry, we write out exactly what we're looking for a person to do to fill this job. We call them job cards. We have job descriptions for our nursery caregivers and our team leaders, and we also fill out job cards and have them readily available. Let me give you an example:

"Our nursery team was brainstorming one day and decided we'd like to find someone to interview our nursery caregivers and write articles for our church newsletter. We were thinking it'd be great to have our caregivers share their experiences of seeing God at work in this ministry area. No team member had the time or the passion for this new ministry area, so we had to look elsewhere for someone to take on this aspect of the ministry. We made a job card, which included the following information:

- ❏ length of the articles
- ❏ questions to include in the interviews
- ❏ a few names (with phone numbers) of people to call
- ❏ contact person (someone on our nursery team) to call with questions
- ❏ deadline information (the date by which they needed to turn in the articles to the church office).

"We had the information, then, to give to the person who accepted this part of the ministry," Jackie continued. "It may sound simple, but I used to dream up lots of jobs, but I'd never write them out specifically. If I happened to find someone who was willing to do the job, I was winging it in terms of letting them know the scope of the job. The result too often was that only half the job got done, and I ended up having to finish many jobs. When I started using the job card approach, I discovered that I rarely have to finish jobs now. When people accept a job card, they know the expectations from the outset, and it helps them feel confident and take ownership in their part of the ministry. Being able to incorporate different people with different gifts—it's exciting and freeing when it happens, and I pray you'll experience this in your nursery ministry, too!"

Claire's ministry team was delighted and encouraged. They set the date for the next nursery ministry team meeting—in two weeks. Claire and Jackie agreed on a time to get together to prepare. Claire left the church that day feeling energized. Jackie's presentation had sparked her thinking, and her mind was racing with ideas. Before leaving the parking lot Claire jotted down a few more ideas in her notebook. It was clear that God was at work, giving Claire the ideas. In the appendixes you'll find some of these additional resources—including job descriptions for team leaders and nursery caregivers, sample interview questions for caregivers, a sample ministry application and release form, a nursery staff evaluation survey, a list of guidelines for nursery use, a sample nursery information card, a sample nursery check-in sheet, a list of suggested contents for diaper bags, a sample nursery cleaning list, and a sample incident report form.

QUESTIONS FOR REFLECTION AND DISCUSSION

1. What is the difference between the responsive approach and the proactive approach to implementing policies? Are there any new policies you should proactively develop in your church nursery? If so, take some time to brainstorm, following the bulleted list on page 43.

2. Look over the job descriptions and forms in the appendixes. Do you see any gaps in what is currently available in your nursery? Do you see any ideas on how you could improve your nursery's existing job descriptions and forms?

SIX

Recruiting the People You Need to Staff Your Nursery

Claire and Jackie met to prepare for Claire's next nursery team meeting, which would be devoted to the topic of recruiting. Claire was grateful for Jackie's help. They planned a team effort—Jackie would lead the discussion on screening and background checks for nursery caregivers, and Claire would lead the discussion on the approach to recruiting. The following is a combination of Jackie's and Claire's notes from the meeting.

RESOURCES FOR BACKGROUND CHECKS, SCREENING, AND TRAINING

❑ Church Law and Tax Report (Matthews, North Carolina) publishes a textbook titled *Reducing the Risk of Sexual Abuse in Your Church: A Complete and Practical Guidebook for Prevention and Risk Reduction,* written by Richard R. Hammar, Steven W. Klipowicz, and James F. Cobble Jr. There is a complete kit available that includes a two-part video, an audiocassette, a leader's guide, and a copy of the textbook. The book and companion materials provide the critical guidance and training a church needs in order to respond to child sexual abuse and helps churches develop an effective abuse prevention program. Contact Church Law and Tax Report at 1-800-222-1840; http://www.ChurchLawToday.com

❏ *Safe Place* is a training book that includes CD-ROM and reproducible forms. Contact Christian Publications, Inc., at 1-800-233-4443; http://www.christianpublications.com

❏ Joy Thornburg Melton has written a book titled *Safe Sanctuaries: Reducing the Risk of Child Abuse in the Church* (Nashville: Discipleship Resources, 1998). This book offers suggestions, sample forms, an implementation plan, and information for training sessions. Contact Discipleship Resources at 1-800-685-4370; http://discipleshipresources.org

❏ Beth Swagman has written a booklet titled *Preventing Child Abuse: A Guide for Churches* (Grand Rapids: Faith Alive Christian Resources, 1997). She guides churches through the process of designing and implementing the policies and procedures they need in order to keep their children safe. Includes screening procedures for volunteers and staff, guidelines for handling abuse allegations, and many helpful appendixes. Contact Faith Alive Christian Resources at 1-800-333-8300; http://www.faithaliveresources.org

❏ Accufax is a respected provider of volunteer and employee background reports to churches in the United States. For more information, call 1-800-256-8898 or 918-627-2226; http://www.accufax-us.com (http://www.accufax-us.com/voluntr.htm).

❏ The GuideOne Center for Risk Management (http://www.guideonecenter.com) hosts an insurance website with sample policies and procedures, fact sheets with suggestions for prevention, and response guidelines, available in a free, downloadable PDF format.

❏ David Dingledy is an educator consultant who leads seminars and training sessions in "Reducing the Risk." He can be contacted at 781-767-3018 or by e-mail at daveding19@aol.com

❏ Dr. Dayl Hufford and Dr. John Mokkosian from the New England Pastoral Institute are available to lead seminars and training sessions on "Safe Church." They can be contacted at 603-890-6767; http://www.nepastoral.org

IMPLEMENTING SAFETY AND PREVENTION POLICIES

If you've never used an application form or a screening process for people who work with children at your church, implementing new policies will be a *huge* change, and it will take time and attention over a significant time span. Be aware that the very thought of having a prevention policy in a church situation is offensive to some people from the outset.

Since the issue of preventing abuse of any kind is a sensitive topic, understand that the issue brings up strong emotions. People often react out of fear or panic ("I don't want anything to happen to my child") and anger ("Why do you have to check my background? I've been a faithful, active member here for twenty-five years, and if you can't trust me without having my social security number, then I guess you don't need me to serve in the nursery").

JACKIE'S TIDBITS OF ADVICE

❏ Revisit notes on the *proactive approach* to implementing policies (page 43). Don't be a lone ranger. Find ways to enlist a broad cross section of people to think through and gather information about this issue.

❏ It is important to help everyone in your church focus on the major issue—*the safety of children.* The issue is not whether or not we trust people; what is crucial is that we take precautions wherever possible in order to create a safe environment for the children.

❏ Attorneys generally note that it is important not to put anything in writing that you cannot realistically implement. From a legal standpoint, it is worse to have policies and procedures in writing when you do not have structures and people in place to implement them. To minimize your risk and to exercise proper caution, be sure to check with your own church attorney on these matters.

JACKIE'S PLEA

Jackie shared passionately with Claire's ministry team her heart for the children served in the nursery ministry:

"Please listen carefully. We all agree that we want to make sure our children are safe. We agree that we want our children to grow up valuing the community—the family of God we call the church. The issue of developing and implementing strategies to provide a safe environment for children has caused much pain for people. Why? Because members of the church family began disagreeing and bickering about the best ways to implement safety policies to protect children. We as adults forget how smart children are. While they may not understand the exact issue the adults are fighting about, they sense when adults aren't truly showing love for each other.

"Think about it for a moment. The whole point of these policies is for the benefit of the children. You see my point, right? Let the process be honoring to God and encouraging for all involved. It will mean lots of prayer for patience as you listen to people. It will mean allowing time for your church family to embrace the need for implementing policies and for praying for the protection of children. The policy isn't a magic wand that will automatically make everything perfect. It reflects the church's commitment to have *everyone* contributing to the atmosphere and structure of safety for the children."

PEOPLE RESOURCES: WHAT KIND OF COMMITMENT DO WE SEEK?

A recurring debate in churches is whether to have nursery caregivers serve on an every-week basis or on a rotating basis of some kind. Here are some questions to use as a guide in developing your approach in recruiting:

- ❏ What are the benefits of having nursery caregivers on a weekly basis?
- ❏ What are the potential pitfalls of having nursery caregivers on a weekly basis?
- ❏ What are the benefits of having nursery caregivers on a rotating basis?
- ❏ What are the potential pitfalls of having nursery caregivers on a rotating basis?
- ❏ What is the best scenario for ministering with children?
- ❏ What is the best scenario for ministering to parents?

❏ What is your church's current practice? What important steps could you change if your expectations for nursery caregivers change?

PEOPLE RESOURCES: WHOM DO WE SEEK?

Here are several questions to use as a guide for recruiting nursery caregivers for your church's nursery ministry:

❏ What are the benefits of asking parents to serve as caregivers?

❏ What are the potential pitfalls of asking parents to serve as caregivers?

❏ What are the benefits of asking non-parents to serve as caregivers?

❏ What are the potential pitfalls of asking non-parents to serve as caregivers?

❏ What kind of person are we looking for—a Christ-follower who loves children, etc.?

❏ What structures do we have in place in order to encourage our caregivers in their relationship with God as they serve in this ministry?

JACKIE'S INSIGHTS ON RECRUITING

Claire shared with the group the practical tips for recruiting that Jackie had passed on to her as they prepared for the meeting.

Before You Pick Up the Phone

❏ Pray for the Holy Spirit to prepare the hearts of the people you're calling.

❏ Pray for God's wisdom and discernment to fill you as you talk with people about opportunities to serve.

❏ Pray that you will be prepared emotionally and mentally for both the yes answers and the no answers.

❏ Review a list of ministry descriptions and opportunities.

❏ Ask a friend to pray with you about these ministry calls.

When You Make the Call

Ask people if it's a good time to talk for a few minutes. If not, ask about a better time to call back.

Some people may just need to talk. Remember that these recruiting phone calls are *ministry opportunities*. God may be prodding you to be an encouragement and bright spot in their day instead of seeking to gain a definite commitment for ministry.

People need time to think and pray. Let them know you will call them back in a week to check in regarding their decision.

We don't want to pressure people into ministry. There are, however, a multitude of ministry opportunities, such as greeting, substituting, and working in the nursery weekly or on a rotating basis. We do want to invite people to be involved in a way that suits their giftedness and passion.

Don't forget to also ask dads how they can become involved.

Take lots of notes so you can remember conversations. It's helpful to have a record of the whys or why-nots, as well as any recommendations for further follow-up.

Need Help Getting Started?

❏ Hi, I'm Samantha from First Church. I don't believe we've met yet, but I was wondering if you have a few minutes to talk about what's happening in the Children and Families Ministry area for the next year. Did you receive the letter from our nursery ministry team regarding the various positions? Are there any ministry opportunities you'd like to know more about? Do you have any questions about our ministry I could answer, or find out the answer and call you back? We're excited about involving some parents and others who don't have children, so we wanted to check to see how you may see yourself joining with us.

❑ Hi, I'm Rachel from First Church. I have a note here that you're interested in helping out in our nursery ministry. That's terrific! I wanted to ask you about your preference for ministry in the next year—which hour, which age group, and so forth.

Follow Up with Those Who Connect Back with You

❑ You've talked extensively with someone about a ministry opportunity. Now this person has called back and left a message. Celebrate the fact that she's taken the time to connect back, and be sure to respond—even if the answer is no. Deliberately thank her for returning the call.

❑ In addition to making a return phone call, write a follow-up note to those who leave a message indicating that they cannot be involved at the present time. Let them know you appreciate that they reflected on the opportunity *and* that they took the time to let you know their decision.

Your Tone of Voice Makes a Difference

❑ If you're excited about what you see God doing in the ministry and you call to ask someone about getting involved, they'll be able to hear the excitement and energy in your voice. If, on the other hand, you've already made fifteen calls with no response and you're tired and frustrated, people will be able to hear that in your voice, too—and it's contagious.

❏ When making a round of recruiting calls, be sure to take breaks in order to maintain perspective. Remember that the call itself is valuable ministry that involves sharing the vision of the ministry, getting people excited about what God is doing, and encouraging someone you may or may not know very well.

❏ When you become weary, take a break and call a friend. Ask him or her to pray for you to maintain focus and perspective. Or consider reading a chapter in a book that you know will be energizing for you. Do whatever is necessary to keep yourself from becoming discouraged and burning out.

QUESTIONS FOR REFLECTION AND DISCUSSION

1. What type of screening do you carry out for your nursery workers and nursery ministry leaders? As a result of what you've read here, what improvements could you make?

2. If you were being asked for the first time to serve in the nursery ministry of your church, how would you appreciate being approached? What are your church's present plans for recruiting nursery workers? Are there specific things you'd like to suggest to improve recruitment in your church?

SEVEN

Establishing What Children Can Learn at Each Level

Jackie sent Claire a "ministry care package" that included a few thoughts and charts to use in her nursery ministry. This chapter includes some of the things Claire found particularly helpful.

ORGANIZING AGE GROUPS FOR SUCCESS

Depending on the space available and the number of children to be served, there are several options to consider with regard to structuring your church nursery by age divisions:

Option 1 has four age divisions: (1) babies, (2) toddlers, (3) twos, and (4) threes. Option 2 has three age divisions: (1) babies, (2) toddlers and twos, and (3) threes. Option 3 has two age divisions: (1) babies, toddlers, and twos, and (2) threes. Option 4 has all ages together—babies, toddlers, twos, and threes.

Jackie gave several suggestions to help plan the organization of the nursery:

❑ Find out the "age of kindergartners" cutoff date for schools in your area.
❑ Try to align dates so that preschoolers will be with their class when they begin school.
❑ When children are two years old, move them to a different division only once a year if possible.

❑ Be sure to communicate to parents what the divisions are and approximately when their children will move between the divisions.

CHILDREN LEARN THROUGH EXPERIENCES

Jackie included a note to Claire in which she wrote, "Often we associate learning with teaching or telling someone something. However, just as adults learn through life experiences, we've also come to see that children learn through life experiences. Being in God's house at an early age is a life experience for young children. Babies and young children quickly learn whether church is a safe and loving place. Hopefully they will learn that it's a place where adults treat each other with love and respect. Though children can't verbalize what they are learning through these experiences, it becomes part of their repertoire of memories. They may not remember specifically what they experienced in the church nursery, but they may well recall the atmosphere that created a sense of trust and security. Children associate these memories and experiences of being in God's house with their understanding of who God is. There is, of course, no perfect church. However, when God's people are committed to following the principles of his Word and living out their faith within the community in genuine, true-to-life ways, even young children sense this."

SOME THOUGHTS ABOUT SEPARATION ANXIETY

Separation anxiety is an exaggerated fear a child feels when she or he is separated from a parent. It typically occurs between the ages of nine months and three years. Although this fear is part of a healthy child's pattern of development, it can be difficult for the child—and can cause emotional stress for parents.

Jackie shared several tips to help make separating from a child easier for both parent and child:

❑ Make frequent trips to the nursery room where your child is cared for. The more familiar she is with the surroundings, the easier it will be to say good-bye to you.

❑ Do not prolong the good-bye. Tell your child good-bye once, and say that you will return for him. Then leave promptly.

❑ Do not sneak away from your child. It can cause more anxiety and can lead her to distrust you.

❑ Understand that your child is learning a valuable lesson: trust. Each time you leave and return, he learns to trust you more.

❑ Enjoy your time in the adult education class or in the worship time. It is a time for you to be encouraged, challenged, and energized in your faith and in your relationship with God.

AGE CHARACTERISTICS CHARTS

These charts will help identify some of the important characteristics of children from the age of six months through the age of five. Use the information in these charts to organize your nursery for successful ministry to these precious members of your church.

6 to 8 Months

My Senses	My Body	Communication	Thoughts	Watch Me, I Like ...
I love the exciting and also messy experience of learning to feed myself.	I have a whole new perspective on the world because I can sit up by myself and also crawl.	I really like imitating you and will let you know I want you to play by using some gestures.	Even though I'm sociable with my family, strangers may make me somewhat anxious.	I'm really wild about bending my legs and pushing off, and also having you bounce me on your knee.
I can drink from a cup, and I'm used to holding a spoon.	Eventually I'll pull myself up to stand, if I can lean on something or on you!	In the midst of my constant babbling and jabbering you'll hear me say "ah, da, ba, ma, di" or "mu."	I love to examine things carefully and I can stay focused.	It's so exciting when you take me grocery shopping.
I'm interested in the sounds objects make—from the sound of crinkling paper to airplanes overhead.	You might find me crawling upstairs, but I might have trouble coming back down.	In addition to my very own name, you'll be surprised by how many words I understand.	I can find things that are hidden behind other things, and I particularly enjoy playing simple hide-and-seek games.	I love repeating activities such as dropping, banging, and knocking over blocks.
I really like to smell different smells, like food cooking, bath powder, and flowers.	Watch me roll a ball and shift objects from hand to hand.			Peek-a-boo and patty-cake help me practice my growing abilities—and they're fun, too!

9 to 11 Months

My Senses	My Body	Communication	Thoughts	Watch Me, I Like …
Music inspires me to sway, hum, bounce, and sometimes Rock Out!	Now I'm a creeper, crawler, scaler, and a climber—a kind of "cruisin' baby."	I will imitate gestures, facial expressions, and also sounds to get the attention I desire.	I can follow one-set directions, and I may surprise you by being able to remember a game we played yesterday.	Pouring, filling, and dumping things in and out of containers is really pleasurable work.
You may see me searching for my favorite blanket or a special toy.	I'm able to stand with a little support, and I can walk if you hold on to both of my hands.	I'm sensitive to others and can express many moods, from sad or angry to happy (my favorite mood).	If you ask me where my eyes are, I can point to them, plus some other parts of my body.	I like to give hugs and kisses, as well as flirt with myself in the mirror.
I can grasp things really well these days, and you'll find me pointing and poking with my index finger.	I can hold two different toys at one time, one in each hand.	I need to be where the action is, and even on occasion I can be a real show-off.	I know the cause of some things, like if I throw a ball, I understand that it will bounce.	I adore riding on Dad's shoulders and also exploring his pockets.
I like the challenge of trying to get both my hands to work together.	You may find me waving bye-bye.	I really like to make clicking sounds with my tongue and say "ma-ma" and "da-da."	I'm beginning to plan ahead and can guess what's going to happen next.	I love going on outings and drives in the family car.

12 to 14 Months

My Senses	My Body	Communication	Thoughts	Watch Me, I Like . . .
Textures and new sensations are like grand adventures, especially with food.	I can do two things at once. Watch me wave, stop, back up, or carry toys while I walk.	More than ever I'm very interested in the things adults do and what they say.	I'll try to figure out how things go together, and I can stack blocks.	It's wonderful to explore drawers, empty cabinets, sort through containers, and stack stuff.
I can reach for toys and objects and grasp them, even while I'm looking away.	I can crawl up the stairs and scoot down all by myself these days.	If you ask "where's Mommy?" I'll go look for her.	I can identify most animals in books and magazines.	You probably won't understand this, but tearing up magazines is one of my favorite activities.
Water play, bath time, splashing, and learning to swim are so exhilarating.	I fully enjoy pushing, pulling, tossing, and flinging actions.	I say "uh-oh" and can use b, c, d, g, words like ball, cat, dog, and go.	I understand that different objects are used for different things.	Please give me some rhythm instruments, finger paints, large crayons, hammer toys, dolls, picture books, and my very own chair.
I'm getting pretty handy. I can scribble and use things like a hairbrush.		I often shout to get your attention.	I find some things that people do or say very silly or funny and laugh out loud.	

15 to 17 Months

My Senses	My Body	Communication	Thoughts	Watch Me, I Like …
I can be more cooperative while dressing. I'm able to take off my socks and hat, and even put my hat back on!	Even though I can walk alone, I still need help keeping my balance at times.	I'm starting to form my first sentences, like "Go bye-bye."	I can match a round peg with a round hole.	I love to role-play and have fun with touching games like "Where's Daddy's nose?"
I like to show you things of interest in books by pointing to them.	I enjoy squatting or kneeling and find it amusing to bend over and peek up through my legs.	I use my hands with my words to get my point across.	I love to identify familiar pictures and books and turn two to three pages at a time all by myself.	I like riding, pushing, and playing with big toys, especially carts and buggies.
I enjoy dipping morsels or scooping food and can feed myself with a spoon.	I climb on furniture and probably can get out of my crib all by myself.	I jabber away, and you may hear me hum my first song.	I can solve a simple problem like "find the kitty."	Chasing games and dancing to music are two of my favorite ways to spend the afternoon.
	I can stop, stoop, pick up a toy, and throw it. I'm getting ready for the Toddler League.	I'm becoming a social butterfly and like to play alongside other babies.		

2-Year-Olds

Because 2-Year-Olds ...	We ...
are active but tire easily ...	alternate quiet with active learning activities and plan learning activities in which they can move.
are timid and easily frightened ...	give them plenty of pats and hugs, carefully planning an orderly, secure class atmosphere.
have a short attention span ...	change activities frequently or have many things from which they can choose.
have a limited vocabulary ...	use simple words and present simple concepts they can understand, defining new words and explaining new concepts.
are literal thinkers ...	are careful to try to teach only concrete concepts, avoiding abstract ones.
have limited experiences ...	relate new concepts to their experiences to facilitate understanding.
do not remember as well as older children ...	repeat simple concepts throughout the class period, using a variety of methods.
are self-centered ...	teach them about sharing and showing consideration for others.
are developing large-muscle control ...	don't expect them to be adept at abilities that require fine motor skills (like cutting around circles).

3-Year-Olds

Physical	Emotional	Spiritual	Social	Intellectual
• move constantly, developing their large muscles with walking and running • have quick bursts of energy and then tire easily • develop hand skills with activities such as building with blocks	• act at a feeling level • respond to emotions adults display • are now becoming sensitive to the way others act	• understanding of spontaneous prayer, not formal prayer • understand God's love by the way parents love them • understand God by the way people treat each other rather than by what people say about God	• prefer to play alone • lack social skills, may push another child to get the child to play • self-centered, need work on taking turns and cooperating	• don't understand symbolism • understand only one direction at a time • have short attention spans, usually around three minutes

4-Year-Olds

Physical	Emotional	Spiritual	Social	Intellectual
• coordination improves; begin jumping, climbing, and skipping	• develop a sense of humor	• understand that praying means talking to God	• seek the approval of adults	• have short attention span, usually around four minutes
• small muscles begin to develop; learn to tie shoelaces, zip, and button	• are sensitive to adults' moods and actions	• understand God's love by the way others express love to them	• want to spend more time with others and less by themselves	• are curious, asking how, what, and why frequently
• are active but tire easily; may kick or hit others	• test limits and rules; throw tantrums	• ask questions about God	• lots of imaginary play experiences with other children	• learn by doing and experiencing their five senses

5-Year-Olds

Physical	Emotional	Spiritual	Social	Intellectual
• becoming more coordinated, agile, and strong • need lots of room to run, hop, jump, and move around • develop hand skills; can cut large objects and almost color within the lines	• thrive on the attention of other peers and adults • feel proud when praised for doing something well • feel self-conscious when they are compared to other children	• understand that God made them • articulate God's love by doing kind things for others • notice when adults say one thing about God and then act differently	• tattle on others to get attention • prefer playing with two or three children instead of in large groups • want to play games that other kids are playing or mimic activities they see adults do	• have an attention span of around five minutes • can carry out a list of instructions • triple vocabulary within one year, from about 1,500 words (age 4) to 5,000 words (age 5)

WHERE TO GO FROM HERE

A couple of months after Claire received the care package from Jackie, they got together again. They met for coffee to catch up on what had been going on in their lives. Over steaming cups of cappuccino, Claire told Jackie what God had been doing through the nursery ministry over the past two months. Claire's church was growing, and members were feeling more and more comfortable inviting their friends with babies to visit. A teacher in an adult education class had told Claire that a married couple—new Christians—began attending church but had concerns about leaving their baby in the nursery during worship. Now they were coming to both Sunday school and worship time because they felt comfortable with the nursery! "Jackie," declared Claire, "it's definitely a testimony to how God has worked in our nursery team."

They went to get their mugs refilled and settled back in their comfortable chairs. "Claire," said Jackie, "someone left a message on my answering machine seeking help with her church nursery." Looking intently at Claire, she said, "I want to challenge you again. I think you're ready to walk alongside someone to encourage, pray for, and invest in her as a ministry partner—just like you and I have been doing. You have a model now. You know how we've walked together in the process, and now you can adapt the process for someone else. What do you think? Are you ready?"

Claire paused. "Well, I think it's something I can do—but it's only through God's strength and because God used you to encourage me and to show me how to encourage others in ministry. So, yes, I'm ready. What's her name and phone number?"

QUESTIONS FOR REFLECTION AND DISCUSSION

1. What are the present age divisions used in your nursery program? Is this working well, or should you consider some of the other options mentioned in this chapter?

2. How do you communicate with parents what the divisions are and approximately when their children will move to another division?

3. Describe any experiences you've had in dealing with separation anxiety among the children in your nursery. What has worked best to deal with this kind of situation?

4. What might be some reasons why it could be helpful from time to time to consult the charts that outline the characteristics of various ages?

5. As a result of working through this book, what action steps would you like to take? Do you know of anyone else who could benefit from reading this book?

APPENDIX 1

Nursery Team Leader Job Description

As a nursery team leader, your role is crucial in communicating to nursery caregivers the importance of their ministry role in the church family. Nursery caregivers help to lay a firm foundation of faith in the lives of babies and toddlers. In a real sense, nursery caregivers, along with parents, are the first picture children see of God and his love for them.

Qualifications

❑ Mature, growing Christian with a love for babies and toddlers
❑ A knowledge of (or a willingness to learn about) baby and toddler characteristics
❑ Dependable and willing to serve on a regular basis
❑ Friendly, cheerful, and capable of developing and getting along with a team

Responsibilities

1. Arrive fifteen to twenty minutes before the session begins so you're there when other caregivers arrive. Help prepare the room as necessary (put sheets on cribs, turn on soft music, organize check-in materials, etc.).

2. Give a warm welcome to parents and babies and toddlers. You are the point person in this transition time. Keep track of information-card use, check-in sheet, and parent communications.

3. Be sure that diaper bags and other belongings are marked with the child's name.

4. Encourage caregivers to regularly check for diaper change needs and to be aware of signs of hunger or discomfort.

5. When babies and toddlers are gone, work with caregivers to follow clean-up procedures.

6. Attend and help lead (as necessary) training meetings.

7. Encourage nursery caregivers to get to know parents and to pray for them and their children. Take time to get to know nursery caregivers and pray for them and encourage them as they serve in this ministry.

8. Participate on the nursery ministry team by attending team meetings and helping to carry out action plans developed in the meetings.

9. Maintain a list of substitute caregivers. Communicate this list to caregivers.

10. Write notes of encouragement to caregivers who serve with you.

APPENDIX 2

Nursery Caregiver Job Description

You have one of the most important jobs in our church's ministry! You are helping to lay a firm foundation of faith in the lives of the babies and toddlers you care for as you hold, cuddle, change, feed, talk to, and play with them. In a real sense, you, along with parents, are the first picture children will see of God and his love for them.

Guidelines for Caregivers

❑ Caregivers must be a minimum of fourteen years old.

❑ Caregivers may not give medication to any child.

❑ Caregivers must not leave children alone at any time or allow a child to leave the room alone.

❑ Caregivers may not work in the baby and toddler rooms if they are coming down with a cold or have other active illnesses.

❑ Except for caregivers and children, no one else should be in the baby and toddler rooms except under special circumstances authorized by the team leader.

Special Tips for Caregivers

❑ Wash your hands after each diaper change and after wiping a runny nose.

❑ Wear a smock and name tag.

❑ Wash chewed-on toys before giving them to another child.

❏ Try to prevent babies from sharing bottles and pacifiers.

❏ Check a child's bag for diapers before using nursery-provided diapers.

❏ Make sure that each baby's diaper is checked at least once during the session.

❏ If a child becomes frustrated or aggressive, redirect his or her attention to another toy or activity.

❏ Report any biting incident by completing an incident report form and letting parents know what happened.

❏ Keep your attention on the babies and toddlers and not on interacting with other caregivers.

What to Do When You Can't Make Your Scheduled Time

❏ If you know in advance you won't be there, it is your responsibility to call someone on the substitute list to cover for you. Let your team leader know who will fill in for you.

❏ If you get stuck and need help finding a substitute, call your team leader.

❏ If you get sick on Saturday or Sunday, call your team leader or the church office to let them know.

APPENDIX 3

Interviewing Nursery Caregivers

Name of applicant _____

Date of interview _____

Interviewer's Initials _____

Connecting

1. How long have you attended First Church? What brought you here? Do you feel connected in this church family (small group, friends, prayer partners, etc.)?

Connecting with God

2. Tell me about the process you went through in making the commitment to trust in Jesus as your personal Savior. (Share your testimony.)

3. What's your journey and relationship like today? How are you nurturing your relationship with the Lord on a daily basis? (What's your current walk with God like?)

Connecting with the Children & Families Ministry Team

4. What sparked your interest in serving on the C & F team? (Why are you interested in being involved?)

5. From your perspective, what are the ways you can contribute to the team atmosphere in this ministry? What are specific ways you can work toward maintaining the unity of the team—and the entire church family?

Safety

6. As a church—and C & F ministry in particular—we are responsible to partner with parents in discipling children and to maintain a safe environment for them while they are in our care here at First Church. Is there any reason why there would be a concern about you working with children here?

Other notes/questions/follow-up recommended:

_____

_____

_____

_____

_____

_____

_____

_____

APPENDIX 4

Children and Families Ministry Application and Release Form

Thank you for your interest in becoming a part of the Children and Families Ministry team. Your willingness to serve in this work is a testimony to your faith and desire to serve the Lord. Thank you for honestly giving us this sensitive information. We want you to know that the information will be kept confidential and only shared with appropriate pastoral staff when deemed necessary.

Please PRINT or write legibly.

General Information

Last name   First name   Male/Female

Date of birth   City of birth   County   State/Country

AKA and/or maiden name   Social Security number

Phone   Work phone   E-mail

Marital status: married/single/engaged/separated/divorced/remarried/widowed

Work status: homemaker/part time/full time/student   Occupation

Spouse's name   Children's names & ages

Current Address   Street & P.O. Box

City   State   Zip

How long at this address (months/years)?

Previous address   Street & P.O. Box

City   State   Zip

How long at this address (months/years)?

Previous address   Street & P.O. Box

City   State   Zip

How long at this address (months/years)?

Church Information

How long have you regularly attended our church?

Are you a member?

If at our church less than two years, list previous church affiliations, including length of time at each.

List all previous church involvement working in children's ministry (identify church and work).

List any gifts, training, and other factors that have prepared you for serving in children's ministry in our church.

Personal Information

Have you committed to trust and follow Jesus as your personal Savior and Lord?   Yes   No

Please describe your personal spiritual journey to date:

Personal Information (continued)

Why do you feel called to work with children?

_____

_____

What are your biggest concerns or fears about working in this ministry area?

_____

_____

_____

What is one job or task you hope you are never asked to do while serving in children's ministry?

_____

_____

What do you think will be your greatest rewards from working in this ministry area?

_____

_____

References

Please list three people who have known you for at least one year who would be able to attest to your character and to your ability to work with children.

1. Name

Length of time known   Nature of association

Address   City   State   Zip

Home phone   Work phone

2. Name

Length of time known   Nature of association

Address   City   State   Zip

Home phone   Work phone

3. Name

Length of time known   Nature of association

Address   City   State   Zip

Home phone   Work phone

Applicant's Statement

The information contained in this application is correct to the best of my knowledge.	Yes	No
I have attached a copy of my driver's license to this application.	Yes	No
I have read and agree with this church's statement of faith.	Yes	No
Should my application be accepted, I agree to be bound by the policies and procedures of the Children & Families Ministry.	Yes	No

In connection with my application to serve as a volunteer in the ministries of this church, I authorize this church and/or ACCUFAX Div., Southvest Inc., their agent, to solicit background information relative to my identity, to any criminal record history, and to my suitability for serving in a position of trust. I understand that this church may conduct inquiries into my background that may include criminal records, personal references, and other records and reports pertaining to me.

I authorize without reservation, any person, agency, or other entity contacted by this church or ACCUFAX Div., Southvest Inc., their agent, for purposes of obtaining background report information, to furnish the above-mentioned information.

I release this church and/or ACCUFAX Div., Southvest Inc. and their respective employees and all persons, agencies, and entities providing information or reports about me from any and all liability arising out of furnishing any such information or reports.

Signature of Applicant _____ Date _____

APPENDIX 5

Nursery Staff Evaluation Survey

1. I have a clear understanding of the vision of our nursery ministry.
   _____ very clear understanding
   _____ sometimes clear, sometimes not clear
   _____ unclear understanding

2. I have a clear understanding of my purpose as a nursery worker in our ministry.
   _____ very clear understanding
   _____ sometimes clear, sometimes not clear
   _____ unclear understanding

3. I feel appreciated and valued in this ministry.
   _____ very appreciated and valued
   _____ sometimes yes, sometimes no
   _____ not appreciated and not valued

4. I have a clear understanding of when I'm scheduled to serve in the nursery. I know who to call and what to do if for some reason I can't be there.
   _____ very clear understanding
   _____ sometimes clear, sometimes not clear
   _____ unclear understanding

5. Needed supplies are available for me to use whenever I serve in the nursery.
   _____ always
   _____ sometimes
   _____ never

6. We have adequate facilities and equipment for our nursery (rocking chairs, changing tables, swings, etc.).

_____ adequate

_____ somewhat lacking

_____ not adequate

7. Parents have a sense of confidence in the safety of our nursery and the care given there.

_____ true

_____ sometimes true, sometimes untrue

_____ never true

8. I have a clear understanding of the policies and procedures in our nursery.

_____ very clear understanding

_____ sometimes clear, sometimes not clear

_____ unclear understanding

9. Identify the strengths of our nursery ministry:

_____

_____

_____

10. Identify areas where we could improve in our nursery ministry:

_____

_____

_____

APPENDIX 6

Guidelines for Nursery Use

We expect everyone who uses our nursery facilities to follow these guidelines, so that we can best meet the needs of children, be good stewards of our supplies and facilities, and maintain high standards of usage.

Apparel

1. All nursery workers must wear a nursery smock, which will protect their clothing from getting stained and prevent children from getting snagged on buttons, ties, jewelry, etc.
2. All smocks are to be placed in the laundry hamper at the end of the session.

Toys and Furniture

3. There is a basket (marked "clean") you may use to get toys to give to the children.
4. All used toys go into the basket marked "dirty."
5. Wash toys at the end of your session with a designated cleaning solution.
6. All toys will be thoroughly cleaned once a month.

Information Card / Sign-in Sheet / Tagging System

7. Have new parents fill out an information card. Place completed card in the marked box.
8. Have parents label their child's diaper bag, bottles, blankets, etc.

9. Have parents sign in their child and jot down the number that corresponds to the tag number you give them.
10. For safety reasons, do not release a child to a parent without a matching tag. The same parent who drops off the child should pick him or her up, unless otherwise communicated at the initial drop-off time. In the event of a misunderstanding, involve the team leader or nursery coordinator.

Changing Diapers

11. Only female nursery workers may change diapers.
12. All nursery workers must either wear gloves or wash hands before and after changing diapers.
13. First remove the dirty diaper and clean the baby with wipes; then take off the dirty gloves or wash your hands and put a clean diaper on the baby. Then wash your hands again.
14. Place dirty diapers in diaper genie or diaper pail.
15. Spray off the changing counter with designated cleanser after each use.

Caregivers

16. The caregiver-to-child ratio is as follows:

   ❑ Babies: one caregiver to three babies
   ❑ Toddlers: one caregiver to four toddlers

17. There must always be a minimum of two workers in the nursery. No caregiver should be alone with a child.
18. There must always be an adult caregiver in the room. A full team of teenage nursery workers is not acceptable.

Food

19. Only snacks approved by the nursery team may be served to infants and toddlers, unless specifically designated by a parent.
20. Children may not share bottles or snacks that come from home.

APPENDIX 7

Nursery Information Card

Child's name _____

Boy/Girl: _____ Birth date: _____

Parents' name: _____

Parents' address: _____

Phone number: _____

Usual nap time is: _____

Place baby/toddler on: ___ back ___stomach ___ side

Usual time for bottle: _____

Mother will nurse: ___ yes ___no

Things that baby/toddler likes to do: _____

Names and ages of brothers and sisters: _____

_____

Any special instructions? _____

_____

Date information card completed: _____

Date information card updated: _____

APPENDIX 8

Nursery Check-In

Date: _____

Label bottles, pacifiers, and diaper bags.

Claim #	Child's name	Age	Parent's name	Location of parents 9:30 A.M.	Location of parents 11:00 A.M.	Parent's instructions
N21						
N22						
N23						
N24						
N25						
N26						
N27						
N28						
N29						
N30						
-N31						
N32						
N33						
N34						
N35						
N36						

APPENDIX 9

Diaper Bag Contents

- ❏ a small diaper bag or sack that will fit easily on the nursery shelf
- ❏ one or two bottles as needed (please permanently label bottles with your child's first and last name)
- ❏ extra diapers (disposable, please)
- ❏ pacifier (clip-on or labeled)
- ❏ change of clothes
- ❏ baby wipes
- ❏ your child's favorite blanket

Parents, you are requested *not* to bring medicine of any kind. If your child needs any medication at all, it *must* be administered by you. Also, please don't bring personal toys for your child. The nursery is comfortably equipped with toys, blankets, burping cloths, and so forth. It is often difficult to track down the items that personally belong to your child, especially when these items look like the ones that the nursery supplies.

APPENDIX 10

Nursery Cleaning List

These tasks are to be done **after each session:**

- ❏ wipe off tabletops
- ❏ wipe off changing counters
- ❏ put toys away
- ❏ put juice in refrigerator
- ❏ vacuum carpets
- ❏ properly dispose of dirty diapers
- ❏ turn off lights and lock doors

Person responsible _____ Date _____

These tasks are to be done **weekly:**

- ❏ do laundry
- ❏ wash dirty toys

Person responsible _____ Date _____

These tasks are to be done **every two weeks:**

- ❏ buy supplies
- ❏ buy snacks

Person responsible _____ Date _____

These tasks are to be done **monthly:**

- ❏ clean and shampoo carpets
- ❏ wipe off shelves

Person responsible _____ Date _____

These tasks are to be done **yearly:**

❏ wash walls
❏ touch up and paint walls as necessary
❏ wash windows

Person responsible _____ Date _____

APPENDIX 11

Incident Report Form

Name: _____ Phone: _____
Home address: _____
Sex: ❑ M ❑ F   Age: _____ Grade: _____

Time accident occurred:
    Hour _____ ❑ A.M. ❑ P.M. Date: _____

Place of accident (be specific): _____
_____

Injured during a program activity? ❑ Yes ❑ No

Ministry representative: _____ Program: _____

WITNESSES TO ACCIDENT, IF ANY:
Name: _____ Phone: _____
Address: _____

Name: _____ Phone: _____
Address: _____

Cause of accident: _____
_____
_____
_____
_____

Nature of injury (what part(s) of body affected): _____
_____
_____

Action taken: _____

_____

_____

_____

_____

Was a parent/legal guardian or other individual on site?
❑ Yes   ❑ No

Was a parent/legal guardian or other individual notified?
❑ Yes   ❑ No

When: _____

Name of individual notified: _____

How: _____

Signature (Person completing form): _____

Position: _____ Date: _____

Follow-up: _____

_____

_____

_____

_____

Complete form and place in administrator's box.

COPY—Business office   COPY—Program or ministry leader

ZONDERVAN PRACTICAL MINISTRY GUIDES
Paul E. Engle, Series Editor

SERVING AS A CHURCH GREETER
This practical guidebook will help you reach out to people who need to experience the warmth of belonging to a church family. **Softcover (ISBN 0-310-24764-0).**

SERVING AS A CHURCH USHER
Your impact as an usher is enormous both in meeting the needs of people and in keeping the church service running smoothly. **Softcover (ISBN 0-310-24763-2).**

SERVING IN YOUR CHURCH MUSIC MINISTRY
This wise, concise guidebook will help you harness your God-given musical talent as a gift to the body of Christ. **Softcover (ISBN 0-310-24101-4).**

SERVING BY SAFEGUARDING YOUR CHURCH
Church ought to be the safest place on earth. Here's how to fulfill that goal in practical ways, Includes diagrams, checklists, and resources lists. **Softcover (ISBN 0-310-24105-7).**

SERVING IN CHURCH VISITATION
Whether visiting people in their homes, in the hospital, or in a restaurant over a cup of coffee, the simple act of connecting with others is filled with powerful possibilities. **Softcover (ISBN 0-310-24103-0).**

SERVING IN YOUR CHURCH PRAYER MINISTRY
God moves in praying churches in ways that planning and programs alone can't produce. **Softcover (ISBN 0-310-24758-6).**

SERVING IN YOUR CHURCH NURSERY
Whether you're leading your church's nursery ministry, serving in it, or just thinking of getting involved, you will welcome the expert insights, encouragement, and resources this book offers. **Softcover (ISBN 0-310-24104-9).**

Pick up your copies today at your favorite bookstore!

GRAND RAPIDS, MICHIGAN 49530 USA

WWW.ZONDERVAN.COM

We want to hear from you. Please send your comments about this
book to us in care of zreview@zondervan.com. Thank you.

GRAND RAPIDS, MICHIGAN 49530 USA

WWW.ZONDERVAN.COM